FIGHT RIGHT

A Christian Response to Conflict Resolution

ISBN 978-1-949628-10-4
Printed in the United States of America.
10 9 8 7 6 5 4 3 2 1   22 21 20 19

Published by The Pastoral Center, http://pastoral.center.

Developed in partnership with MennoMedia and Brethren Press. Series editors: Fumiaki Tosu, Ann Naffziger, and Paul Canavese. *Fight Right:* Writers, Jim and Kim Yaussey Albright. Project editor, Lani Wright. Staff editors, Susan E. Janzen, Julie Garber, and James Deaton. Updated design, Paul Stocksdale.

All rights reserved. Purchase of this book includes a license to reproduce this resource for use in a single parish, school, or other similar organization. You are allowed to share and make unlimited copies only for use within the organization that licensed it. If you serve more than one organization, each should purchase its own license. You may not post this document to any web site without explicit permission to do so. Outside of these conditions, no part of this book may be reproduced in any form or by any means, electronic or mechanical, including photocopying, recording, taping, or via any retrieval system, without the written permission of The Pastoral Center, 1212 Versailles Ave., Alameda, CA 94501. Thank you for cooperating with our honor system regarding our licenses.

For questions or to order additional copies or licenses, please call 1-844-727-8672 or visit http://pastoral.center.

Portions of this work © 2019 by The Pastoral Center / PastoralCenter.com. Adapted and published with permission from Generation Why Bible Studies. © 1996, 2014 Brethren Press, Elgin, IL 60120 and MennoMedia, Harrisonburg, VA 22803, U.S.A. All rights reserved.

Unless otherwise noted, the Scripture passages contained herein are from the *New Revised Standard Version of the Bible*, copyright © 1989 by the National Council of the Churches of Christ in the United States of America. Used by permission. All rights reserved.

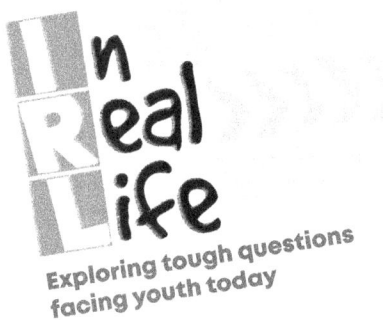

Bible-based Explorations of Issues Facing Youth

>> OVERVIEW

When conversing online, the acronym IRL stands for "in real life." The virtual world of social media, text chats, blogs, and more have the power to remove us from the real world. What we experience online can skew our perspective on what it means to be human. It can numb us, incite us, distract us, depress us, confuse us, and make us rude or impatient. Strangely, this supposedly "social" and "connected" technology can profoundly disconnect us from others.

Religious faith can also place us in a bubble, especially when it distances us from others. When we keep the prophetic message at a safe distance, obscured in theological language and abstractions, we are missing the whole point. And when we see our parish as an insider club that serves itself, we can forget the radically inclusive message entrusted to us: God's love is for *everyone*, and God expects us to transform the *whole world* through that love.

Through the incarnation, God showed up in the real world to show us that our faith is not just about talking the talk, but also walking the walk. It can be risky. It can be confusing. It can hurt. But living out our faith can also bring us great purpose, peace, and joy.

This series connects the Bible with the tough questions that youth (and adults) encounter in their neighborhood, in school, among friends, and even online. This process will help you as a leader break open these issues in a fun and meaningful way, sparking conversation and the kind of life change Jesus invites us to embrace.

>> THE ROLE OF PARENTS

As children enter middle school and high school, they become more independent, self-reliant, and, well, self-centered. This can bring parents to make assumptions that this is the time to step back, giving their child more space to form their identity. While there is truth to that at some level (adolescents definitely shouldn't be smothered), this is a stage of life when parents should in fact *lean in*. The apparent confidence and bluster youth show on the outside can mask the insecurity and confusion on the inside. Youth need their parents to be involved more than ever.

>> WHOLE FAMILY FORMATION

Parents are the primary teachers of their own children, and parishes are waking up to the fact that faith formation programs need to bring parents into the process if they hope to see faith passed on to the next generation. Recent studies give us more and more evidence that the role of parents is the most important factor in determining whether a child will embrace faith as they move toward adulthood. Research from the Center for the Applied Research on the Apostolate shows that parents who talk about their faith and show through their actions that their faith is important to them are more likely to have children who remain Catholic.

More about Whole Family Formation >>>>

To learn more about how your parish can take a comprehensive whole family approach to faith formation, visit **GrowingUpCatholic.com**.

While whole family events with elementary-aged children are on the rise, the role of parents can be an afterthought in youth ministry. We have designed the sessions in this series to work with or without parents present, and we encourage you to offer them as parent-child events.

If you choose to involve parents, it is important to consider before each session how to best do so. Many of the activities in this series are high-energy, creative, or silly. Some parents may need some encouragement to get out of their heads and have fun with the group. A few activities involving physical contact would be inappropriate for parents and youth to participate together, and we have noted them as such.

There are a number of ways to approach discussions with parent participation. Unless you have a small group, you will likely want to break into smaller groups for conversation. Some youth may be self-conscious and unable to be completely honest and open in a group situation with a parent present. For this reason, you may choose in some cases to assign parents to different groups from their own children, or to have separate parent and child groups altogether. Be sure to cover expectations around confidentiality. It is inappropriate for a parent (or youth) to share with another parent what their child said in a small group.

Note that even if parents and their children do not share all conversations together in the session, they will still have a valuable shared experience and can have extended conversations about it later.

>> THANK YOU

The role you play in gathering, animating, praying with, and forming youth is a valuable one. Thank you for all you do to serve the church and its families!

Bible-based Explorations of Issues Facing Youth

FIGHT RIGHT
A Christian Response to Conflict Resolution

>> INTRODUCTION

Why doesn't instruction about the "facts of life" include the nature of conflict? Certainly conflict is an ever-present reality, as natural and inevitable as the rising of the sun in the morning.

Many of us learn at an early age to think of conflict as something bad or dangerous, the opposite of love, harmony, and unity. The reality is that conflict is a necessary part of the most loving, harmonious, and united relationships. People in these relationships have learned that conflicts spring from the fact that people are simply *different*. They have learned to value differences precisely because differences bring excitement and growth to a relationship. To deny conflict is to deny those differences. To deny those differences is to deny people their God-given uniqueness. And to deny that is to take the life out of a relationship. The only place where there is never conflict is the graveyard.

The fact is that conflict at its inception is *neutral*. Whether it becomes a negative force or a positive force depends on how we respond to it. Most dictionary definitions of conflict are decidedly negative: "1. to be contradictory, at variance, or in opposition; clash; disagree. 2. to fight or contend; do battle. 3. a fight, battle, or struggle, esp. a prolonged one; strife." What is being described here is not simply conflict, but conflict that has escalated into a negative force. A more helpful definition is this one: "the interplay of differences between two or more entities acting to meet needs." This accurately reflects the neutrality of conflict, and leaves open the possibility that it can become a positive force. The true opposites of love, harmony, and unity are hate, discord, and division. And the key to whether we live at one end of that spectrum or the other is how we respond to differences and the conflict that rises naturally from them.

Conflict has been a particular problem for Christians. Somewhere along the line the church began to equate "being Christian" with "having no conflicts." After all, we are supposed to love one another, aren't we? But even the Bible is packed with records of conflicts, from Adam and Eve, to Abraham, to Moses, to the prophets, to Jesus himself! Just read the letters in the New Testament—conflict was an ever-present reality in the early church. Most of these conflicts are not simply examples of what we are not supposed to do. No, these conflicts show us that God uses conflict to achieve divine purposes. As peace and conflict mediator Ron Kraybill has pointed out, "Conflict is the arena of God's revelation." One of the most helpful examples for the church today is the story in Acts 15 of the conflict over circumcision. God moved in a council of church leaders who met to discuss the controversy, and the result was the opening of the church to the Gentiles, and the beginning of a new era of witness and growth. Some say, ruefully, that change cannot occur without conflict. What they mean is that conflict is an

>>
CONFLICT:
the interplay of differences between two or more entities acting to meet needs.

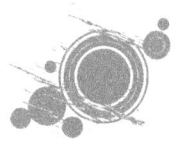

>>> EXTENDER SESSION

Extender sessions suggest special activities related to the issue of the unit. They help accommodate the diversity of parish schedules. Since each unit is undated, participants may study units in their entirety and still participate in special events of the parish that get scheduled simultaneously with youth group time. Extender sessions can be used anytime, but the one for this unit best follows **Session 5**. Calculate now whether or not you will be using the extender session.

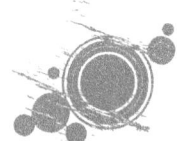

unfortunate side effect of change. The reality is that without conflict there is no change! The greatest example, of course, is Christ crucified. Without the cross there can be no resurrection.

The youth of today are fortunate to live in a time when our understanding of conflict as a positive force is growing by leaps and bounds. The witness of Gandhi, Martin Luther King, Jr., Aung San Suu Kyi in Burma, and Malala Yousafzai, a Pakistani activist for female education and the youngest-ever Nobel Peace Prize recipient, are inspiring examples of conflict as a force for positive change. Yet for most of us, the conflict we experience is in our everyday relationships at home, at work, in school, and at church. But the same principle still applies. These sessions are designed to help participants learn how to respond to conflict with skill and insight, not because conflict is a necessary evil that they need to eliminate, but so that, through an appreciation of differences, they can bring life, excitement, and positive change to their relationships.

When conflict came to a previous generation, they said, "Oh no, not again!" Our hope is that when conflict comes to this generation, they will say, "I wonder what God is trying to tell us now!"

THE SESSION PLAN: The parts of the session guide

>> **Faith story.** The session is rooted in this Bible passage.

>> **Faith focus.** The story of the passage in a nutshell.

>> **Session goal.** The entire session is built around this goal. What changes—in knowledge, attitude, and/or action—do you desire in your group?

>> **Materials needed and advance preparation.** This is what you will need if the session is to go smoothly. You'll feel more at ease if you've taken care of these details before you meet your group.

>> FROM LIFE TO BIBLE TO LIFE

The teaching plan we use is called *life-centered*. However, when we write each session, we always begin with Scripture. We ask, what does this particular passage say, especially to youth? Each session moves from life to Bible to life. So the Bible is really at the center of this way of teaching.

In every session we try to hit upon a tough question participants might ask. Find out what questions on this issue are important for *your* group. By all means, bring your own input and invite your group members to add their own experiences.

TEACHING THE SESSION

The five step-by-step movements will carry you from *life to the Bible and back to life*. Each session takes about 45 to 50 minutes. If there is a handout sheet for the session, take note of any complementary activities and stories.

1. **Focus.** Intended to create a friendly climate within the group and to *draw attention* to the issue.

2. **Connect.** Invites participants to *express* their own life experience about the issue, through talking, drawing, role playing, and other activities. Also uses memory, reason, or imagination to get the group thinking about *why* they view the issue the way they do.

3. **Explore the Bible.** What does the Bible *say* about the issue? With a minimum of lecturing, dig into the faith story and search for answers to questions raised in the first activities. The Insights from Scripture section will help clarify the faith story. Help participants discover how the faith community understands the Bible passage.

4. **Apply** the faith story. What does the Bible passage *mean* for contemporary life? This is the "aha!" moment when participants realize the faith story has wisdom for *their* lives.

5. **Respond.** Why does the Bible passage *matter*? What will the group do about the issue in light of what they have learned from their own experiences set alongside the faith story? How can we *live* the faith story rather than pass it off as a mere intellectual exercise?

LOOK AHEAD

Here are reminders for what you need to do for the next session or two.

INSIGHTS FROM SCRIPTURE

Here is a resource for Explore the Bible. Don't try to use all the material given. Take what you need to lead the session and answer questions your group may have. Let the Insights section inspire you to think and study more about the passage for the session.

HANDOUT SHEETS

Occasionally, there will be a handout sheet to complement your session. If you choose to use this, make enough copies for the group in advance of the session. These sheets may include questions, stories, agree/disagree exercises, charts, pictures, and other materials to stimulate thinking and discussion.

Generally, no participant preparation is required unless the session plan calls for you to contact selected group members for specific tasks.

> "I've learned from that wonderful mother of mine that you've got to learn how to disagree without being disagreeable. That's held me in good stead all my life."
>
> Abraham Lincoln Marovitz, senior judge of U.S. district courts, quoted in Studs Terkel's *Coming of Age*

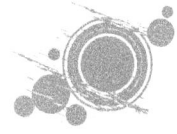

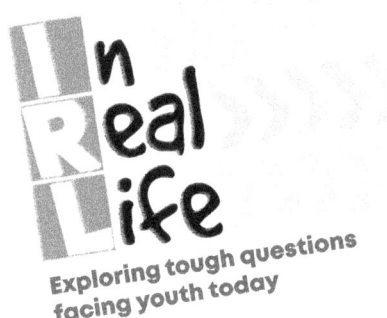

SESSION 1

DIFFERENCES MAKE THE DIFFERENCE! >>>

>>> KEY VERSES

As it is, there are many members, yet one body. The eye cannot say to the hand, "I have no need of you," nor again the head to the feet, "I have no need of you." (1 Cor. 12:20, 21)

>>> FAITH STORY

1 Corinthians 12:12-26

>>> FAITH FOCUS

Conflict is a fact of life. Paul knew it, and so did the Christians in Corinth. For Paul, and for other writers of the Bible, the goal of the faithful life is not to eliminate conflict, but to deal with it in a positive way.

In this passage Paul lays the groundwork for a positive understanding of conflict that can transform how we relate to each other. Using the image of the church as a body, Paul asserts (1) that the very differences that cause conflict are a necessary part of God's creation; (2) that the conflict resulting from differences can be viewed not as something negative, but as a means whereby the Holy Spirit reveals God's will and inspires growth; and (3) that the best way to transform unhealthy conflict into healthy conflict is to acknowledge and celebrate differences for the good of the whole.

>>> SESSION GOAL

Help participants challenge their negative assumptions about differences and open themselves to the positive effects of healthy conflict.

>>> Materials needed and advance preparation

- Chalkboard/chalk or newsprint/markers
- Bibles
- Copies of the handout sheet for Session 1 (see Apply)

TEACHING PLAN

1. FOCUS 7-8 minutes

>>> **Option A:** Ask participants to respond to these true/false statements (possible answers in the sidebar on p. 5) by *standing up*, if they believe the statement is true, and by *sitting on the ground* if they believe it's false. Allow a little bit of time for discussion of each statement and the responses.

»»»
Answers to True/False:

1. True.
But rather than being negative, conflict can lead to positive change.

2. False.
Handled constructively, conflict can strengthen relationships.

3. False.
How we deal with conflict determines the outcome, positive or negative.

4. False. Separating the conflict from the person/group is critical.

5. False. Perceptions of the problem, as well as aspects of right and wrong concerning it, will likely be different anyway.

1. Conflict is a fact of life.
2. Relationships usually get destroyed by conflict.
3. In the end, all conflicts finish in violence.
4. Usually, one can point to a single person or group as the source of a conflict.
5. Figuring out who's right and who's wrong is the most important part of resolving a conflict.

Finally (no true/false on this one), ask participants what words or phrases immediately come to mind when they hear the word "conflict." Have them call them out and quickly list them on newsprint or a chalkboard. Ask the group to make observations about the list. Ask: *How many words or phrases are negative? Are any positive? What does this say about our understandings of conflict? Where do these understandings come from?*

2. CONNECT 12 minutes

Ask for three examples of conflicts that youth might experience. These might include a misunderstanding between friends, classmates, or teammates, a fight between a boyfriend and girlfriend, or an argument with a parent. Ask for volunteers to create "statues" or poses, or make faces, that express their impressions of or emotional reactions to each conflict (or, quickly share phone photos of people reacting to conflict). Ask the group to make observations about what they have seen.

Ask:

1. *Where does the conflict come from in each instance?*
2. *Do these conflicts have anything in common? What?*
3. *How much was the conflict caused by differences between you and the other person or persons in your story?*

As discussion gets going, let participants add other experiences of conflict. In each instance, try to discover where the conflict was caused by differences.

3. EXPLORE THE BIBLE 15 minutes

Shift to the next activity by saying: *It seems that conflicts are primarily caused by differences. If so, why did God create so many differences in the world? Let's see what the Bible tells us....*

Present a list of the following body parts: **Brain, ears, eyes, mouth, stomach, arms, hands, legs, and feet.** Assign participants to represent body parts depending on how many people are in your group:

A. 4-18 people: Pair up and use as many of the body parts as you have pairs.
B. Three or fewer: Have each person choose a body part.
C. More than 18: Divide into groups of three (or more as needed).

The task: *Try to convince the others that your body part is the most important of all.*

Give each individual or group 2 minutes to identify what is most important about their body part from their point of view. Then have everyone come together. Each individual/group gets 3 minutes to try to convince the other groups that their body part is the most important of all.

Then ask: *How did you feel during the Great Body Part Debate?*

Pass out Bibles. Now read 1 Corinthians 12:12-26. Continue the discussion:

1. *Think about the passage, and then say what you think was happening during the debate.*
2. *What, in your own words, does the passage have to say about differences?*
3. *Does the passage identify any one part of the body as the most important?*

4. ### APPLY 15 minutes

Go over the **Conflict Cycle** (handout sheet) with the group. (If your group likes role plays, act out Matthew's response to conflict in the "Going Down" cycle.) Ask: *How does Matthew's response to conflict reinforce a negative view of differences?* Point out how the repetition of the cycle escalates the conflict.

Then ask: *How can we reverse the cycle from a negative cycle to a positive cycle?* (Again, role play Matthew's response to conflict in the "Going Up" cycle, if it helps your group.) Ask: *How does Matthew's response reinforce a positive view of differences?*

5. ### RESPOND 7-8 minutes

Option A: Have participants divide into small groups for the various body parts you listed earlier. Give them 2 minutes to list all the other parts, and brainstorm reasons their *group* body part needs each of the other parts. **OR**, instead of dividing again, share with the group how your body part needs at least one other body part. For example, the "Hand" group may list: "Arm: connects us to body, helps us reach things on top shelf," and so on. Then have them come together and share their reasons with each other. Ask:

1. *How does this exchange feel different from the first one?*
2. *Why does it feel different this time around?*

Option B: Have participants create a new list of words and phrases that describe their response to the word "conflict." Write it on newsprint or a chalkboard. Have them contrast this list with the first list.

Option C: Identify an imaginary line from one end of the room to the other as a continuum, and assign one end as **negative**, and the other as **positive**. Have participants place themselves on the continuum in response to the following statement: *"When I first came to this session this is how I felt about conflict."* Have people who are near each other on the continuum gather in groups of three or four and talk with each other about why they placed themselves where they did. Give an opportunity for each group to sum up their discussion for the large group. Then have them place themselves on the positive/negative continuum in response to this statement: *"This is how I feel about conflict now."* Report to the group as a whole. Help participants identify any insights they received, as well as any questions or anxieties about conflict they still have.

For all options: Sum up by saying something like this: *Conflict is a normal and natural part of life, and arises from our differences. Differences can lead to unpleasant and even painful conflict. But the Bible tells us that differences are a gift of God, and that conflict can be healthy and positive. The next sessions will help us put this truth into action.*

Close with prayer.

HOW CONFLICT AFFECTS US

"Conflicts that go unresolved can damage self-esteem, the ability to trust, and overall outlook on life. Conflicts teach about relationships, trust, life, forgiveness, and ultimately, about God."

Jim Still-Pepper

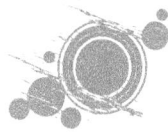

Depending on how we respond to it, conflict can either:
EXCLUDE or INVOLVE
CONFUSE or CLARIFY
ENMESH or DEFINE
DEADEN or STIMULATE
CLOSE or OPEN
DIVIDE or UNITE

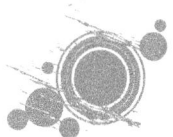

LOOK AHEAD

The next session uses toy or pictorial representations of five specific animals. Gather these. There is also an option to download and administer an inventory to help participants discover their personal response to conflict. Familiarize yourself with the directions for taking and scoring the inventory, if you choose to use it.

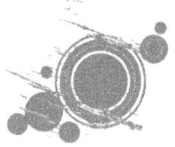

"Though I am different from you, we were born involved in one another."

T'ao Ch'ien

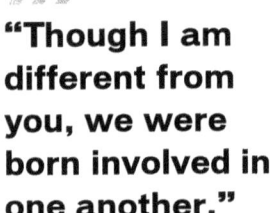

INSIGHTS FROM SCRIPTURE

In this passage we find one of the most fully developed statements of Paul's theology of the church as the Body of Christ. It is sandwiched between a discussion of the meaning of communion and the famous "love chapter."

In 1 Corinthians 11, Paul explains communion as both a memorial to Christ's body broken on the cross, and a ritual act that transforms the community into the Body of Christ. Paul is concerned about the integrity of the Body, and he admonishes some in the church at Corinth, who, through their disregard for others, eat and drink judgment upon themselves, and tear down community. He calls the Corinthians to "discern the body," that is, to be mindful of community in everything they do.

Chapter 13, which immediately follows the metaphors of the parts of the body, ties together for the Corinthian Christians all issues having to do with community—which needs to be understood in the context of sacrificial love. This chapter is powerful on its own, but it has even more power when seen as a continuation of Paul's discussion of community in chapter 12. This was certainly Paul's intention, for he closes chapter 12 with a transition into chapter 13: "And I will show you a still more excellent way."

»» WELCOME TO THE DANCE

The chapter 12 passage, seen in this broader context, is the heart of Paul's understanding of the church as the Body of Christ. Using the image of the human body—one body made up of many parts—he describes the marvelous interplay between diversity and unity. Each needs the other; they are partners in an ongoing dance of community. Diversity without unity is chaos. Unity without diversity is a bland and lifeless uniformity. Furthermore, Paul makes it clear that diversity is not a problem or aberration that unity holds in check or corrects. Diversity is intended by God, and is a necessary component of unity. For Paul, this is most clearly seen in the distribution of different spiritual gifts among the various members of the church. While the gifts are different, they all come from one Source. And, most importantly, the different gifts are given for one and the same purpose: to build up the community of faith. As one commentary puts it: "The common good is served by the contribution of many different types of persons inspired by the Spirit, each possessing a special gift essential to the life of the church" (*The Interpreter's One-Volume Commentary on the Bible*).

»» CONFLICT IS.

Where there are differences, there will be conflict. This leads to a most important and liberating realization: Conflict is not in itself wrong or bad. In 1 Corinthians 6, Paul doesn't scold the Corinthians for having disputes and disagreements. He scolds them for the way they are handling them! *The important thing is how people respond to conflict.* Conflict is initially neutral. Depending on how we respond to conflict, however, it has the power to either break down community, or strengthen community. The goal of community life then, is not to eliminate all conflict; that is neither possible nor desirable. The goal, rather, is to respond to conflict skillfully, expectantly, and redemptively. When we can do that we discover something else: the thread of the Way of God weaving through conflict!

» MAKING THE CONNECTION

Negative or unhealthy conflict develops when individuals lose sight of their own connectedness to the whole. When that happens, differences are perceived as threatening, as a challenge to be overcome. Positive and healthy conflict develops when people understand that their own personal well-being is linked with the well-being of others, and, more importantly, with the well-being of the whole Body.

»»

"Civilization . . . is the acceptance, and the encouragement, of differences."

Mahatma Gandhi

THE CONFLICT CYCLE

How we respond to conflict depends on what we believe about it. Our response always has consequences. Those consequences confirm and reinforce our beliefs about conflict. So the next time conflict occurs we respond in the same way. Like an elevator, the conflict cycle goes in only two directions: up or down.

STAGE ONE: BELIEFS ABOUT CONFLICT
Matthew believes that conflict is a threat to his ability to be successful.

STAGE TWO: CONFLICT OCCURS
Matthew is struggling to keep up in math. Matthew hears that Aaron is making fun of him behind his back, calling him "Stupid."

GOING DOWN
Negative beliefs lead to negative responses, which lead to negative consequences, which reinforce negative beliefs… and the conflict cycle spirals downward.

STAGE FOUR: CONSEQUENCES
Aaron steals Matthew's math book, and Matthew flunks the next math test. He is certain now that everyone thinks he's stupid, and vows to get even with Aaron…

STAGE THREE: RESPONSE TO CONFLICT
Matthew slams Aaron against a locker and threatens to beat him up if he doesn't cut it out.

STAGE ONE: BELIEFS ABOUT CONFLICT
Matthew believes that conflict is an indication that it's time to communicate and gather information, and maybe to learn and grow.

STAGE TWO: CONFLICT OCCURS
Matthew is struggling to keep up in math. Matthews hears that Aaron is making fun of him behind his back, calling him "Stupid."

GOING UP
Positive beliefs lead to positive responses, which lead to positive consequences, which reinforce positive beliefs… and the conflict cycle spirals upward.

STAGE FOUR: CONSEQUENCES
Aaron, who excels in math, explains that he had noticed Matthew's struggle with math, and had said, "It must make Matthew feel really stupid." He apologizes if it hurt Matthew's feelings, and offers to tutor him. Matthew begins to do much better in math….

STAGE THREE: RESPONSE TO CONFLICT
Matthew finds an opportunity to tell Aaron what he heard, and explains how difficult math is for him.

Permission is granted to photocopy this handout for use with this session.

SESSION 2

TRUTH AND LOVE! ~~OR DARE?~~ »

» KEY VERSE
But speaking the truth in love, we must grow up in every way into him who is the head, into Christ. (Eph. 4:15)

» FAITH STORY
Ephesians 4:11-16

» FAITH FOCUS
This passage tells us two things: First, we must speak the truth. That's not easy when we find ourselves in conflict. We even convince ourselves that for the good of the relationship we must not be honest about how we feel or what we think of the conflict.

But the passage goes on to say we can speak the truth *in love*. When love is present, truth-telling will not harm others or our relationship with them, but will instead be the foundation stone for rebuilding the relationship.

» SESSION GOAL
Help participants become aware of their own feelings about conflict, in order to free them to deal with conflict truthfully and lovingly.

» Materials needed and advance preparation

- Copies of the handout sheet for Session 2
- Small animal toys or photos of each of the animals listed on the handout sheet
- Optional: prepare to give a formal conflict styles inventory (see Focus)
- Pencils and writing paper
- Bibles

TEACHING PLAN

1. FOCUS 15 minutes
Distribute copies of the handout sheet, and review them with the group, making sure everyone understands the conflict styles represented. Using toys or visual representations of each animal listed on the sheet, invite each person to pick up a toy or the picture, and say what characteristics about that animal seem *most like them* in how they *typically* deal with conflict.

Note: If you have more than 8 people in the group, divide into smaller groups for this activity, to facilitate more discussion.

>> **Optional:** For a more in-depth self-assessment, download and/or print Ron Kraybill's revised Conflict Style Inventory. Review copies and a free trainer's guide are available on this website:
www.riverhouseepress.com/Conflict_Style_Inventory_Free_Review_Copy.htm.

While similar in concept to the more well-known Thomas Kilmann Conflict Mode Instrument, the Kraybill version has "calm" and "storm" questions to differentiate times when stress or conflict is high (storm) versus more regular interactions (calm). Visit the Riverhouse Press website for a comparison of the two instruments.

Have each person individually complete the inventory, and stress that there are no right or wrong answers, and that the results are not the final word on how they deal with conflict in every setting. This inventory is a tool to help them identify the way they usually respond to conflict. Such self-knowledge can help participants determine what they like about the way they respond, and what they would like to change. Explain that the entire group will discuss the results in general, but assure them that they can keep their own personal results confidential if they wish.

2. CONNECT 20 minutes

After each person has had an opportunity to choose a "conflict style" animal, pick up each of the animal representations in turn and ask:

1. When would this response be appropriate?
2. What happens if you always (avoid, compete, etc.)?

Encourage them to use personal examples if they are willing. This can help people assess the advantages and disadvantages in the various styles.

Now ask, *What do you like about the ways you respond to conflict? What don't you like?*

Invite anyone who wishes to pick up an animal a second time as they respond to the following:

How do you wish you would usually respond to conflict?

3. EXPLORE THE BIBLE 7-8 minutes

Shift to this activity by saying: *The church at Ephesus struggled with how to blend their various conflict styles and come to unity. In Paul's letter to the Ephesian Christians, he reveals the key to unity.*

Read Ephesians 4:11-16 by going around the group and inviting each person to read one verse (or to "pass"). Then ask:

1. What is the key to unity?
2. What does it mean to "speak the truth in love"?
3. Have you seen this in our own church/your home/school? When?

4. APPLY 5 minutes

Referring to the handout sheet again, point out the placement on the graph of each of the five responses. Explain that the vertical axis represents *Assertiveness*, and measures the degree of concern for personal goals, while the horizontal axis represents *Cooperation*, and measures the degree of concern for the relationship.

Then say: *The Bible passages from Ephesians encourage us to "speak the truth in love." When we apply that to this graph, we can see that the healthy balance of assertiveness and cooperation depends on the healthy balance of truth and love. We need to be **assertive** in expressing the **truth** in a conflict setting by being honest about how we feel and what we need. Such assertiveness can be loving. But if we're too assertive, we could hurt or alienate others. So we also need to **cooperate** as another way to show **love** by taking into consideration the feelings and needs of others, even those with whom we are in conflict.*

Now ask: *What do you think is the healthy balance of truth and love when you are in a conflict with someone? How much does it depend on the kind of conflict, or who the conflict is with? What observations do you have about this interplay of truth and love in your own life: at home, at school, at work, at church?* Give time for discussion.

LOOK AHEAD

For the next session you want to be thoroughly familiar with the communication skills outlined on the handout sheet for Session 3.

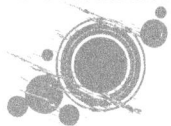

5. RESPOND 7-8 minutes

Optional: Show the following YouTube video about a program of On Earth Peace specifically for training youth to transform conflict:
Agape Satyagraha (https://youtu.be/m1bP20hOJxw).

For practice, offer the following 2 scenarios:

1. You and Josh are co-leaders of a group. Josh hasn't been doing his share, leaving you with most of the work. You're already frustrated, and when your supervisor asks you what's going on you get downright angry. In this situation, what would it mean to speak the truth in love?

2. In the hallway before a youth meeting, you and Jill have a fight. Before you can settle anything it's time for the meeting. All through the meeting, you and Jill don't even look at each other. But after the meeting, you see Jill coming toward you, still obviously angry. When she reaches you, how would you speak the truth in love?

Now, give each person a piece of paper and have them divide it into two columns. Label the first column "Truth" and the second "Love." Then say: *Think of a conflict in your own life right now. Write in column one what is true about that situation by completing several phrases beginning with "The truth is...."* You might write, for example, "The truth is I'm afraid to say how I really feel," or "The truth is I was wrong to jump to conclusions." Be as thorough as possible.

When each person has completed column one, say: *Now in column two identify the ways you can be more loving as you acknowledge and perhaps speak the truth in that situation by completing several phrases beginning with "Speaking the truth in love means...."* You might write, for example, "Speaking the truth in love means letting him/her know how I really feel even though it feels vulnerable" or "The truth is I jumped to conclusions before having enough information because I wanted to believe a certain thing." When each one has finished, say: *Take this paper with you this week (or take a phone photo of it) as a personal covenant to speak the truth in love.* Close with prayer.

MEDIATION RESOURCE

Another resource for mediation training is the Catholic Mobilizing Network. See
https://catholicsmobilizing.org/find-circle-trainer.

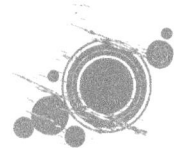

In Real Life | Fight Right   17

 INSIGHTS FROM SCRIPTURE

This passage from Ephesians is concerned with the unity of the church. The author lists several of the gifts of the Spirit (compare 1 Corinthians 12 and Romans 12) in order to emphasize that unity is not *impaired* by diversity, but rather *depends* on it. The point is that *unity is not uniformity*, in which individual differences are discouraged. Rather, it is a distribution of a wide range of gifts among the many members of the body, each of which is essential for the welfare of the whole.

〉〉 GROW UP!

The author sees the attainment of unity as a process of spiritual growth from childishness to maturity. In this view, spiritual immaturity is the most serious threat to unity in the church. This immaturity is characterized by the lack of a spiritual center. That apparently was what some believers at Ephesus were missing. They tended to be "tossed to and fro and blown about by every wind of doctrine, by people's trickery, by their craftiness in deceitful scheming" (Eph. 4:14). Such a state of affairs undermines and prevents unity.

The "cure" is to speak the truth in love! In this context, the author is talking about two levels of relationship. On the one hand, there are our relationships within the faith family. The author has clearly been around churches long enough to know that when people suppress the truth and repress their feelings in hopes of preventing conflict, the opposite happens—conflict explodes! Speaking the truth in love can prevent that by keeping conflicts out in the open where they can be dealt with. Risking enough to speak the truth develops trust, trusting one another lays the groundwork for Christian love, and loving one another creates mutual respect which compels us to speak the truth to one another, thus continuing the building up of unity.

On the other hand, the author is talking about our relationship with the Spirit. The Spirit is love, and the Spirit is truth. To speak the truth in love is nothing less than submitting to the leading of the Spirit. Acting alone, we are simply unable to discern the truth of a situation, or to love someone we are in conflict with. We need the Spirit, and we need the community of faith to help us overcome our selfishness and insecurities. To admit that, and depend on the guidance of the Spirit, is a mark of spiritual maturity.

THE KEY TO GROWING COMMUNITY

Here is the key, then: The more spiritually mature we are, the more we will be centered in the Spirit. For the author, this centeredness is much more than an inward, personal experience of the Spirit, as though the Spirit could be packaged into individual servings like frozen dinners. Rather, the Spirit calls us to a loaded banquet table with unlimited place settings, so that together we might enter into deep fellowship with one another. When we experience that kind of community, we discover a miraculous thing: Christ is in our midst! Not only that, but the community of faith becomes Christ's Body! The community of faith then becomes the actual center of a Christian's spiritual life. No wonder it is so important to care for our relationships with one another by speaking the truth in love!

So speaking the truth in love is both the way we grow in our relationships with our brothers and sisters, and the way we grow together to be the Body of Christ. In other words, it's the way we grow up! The *Interpreter's Bible* sums it up this way:

> "The way of truth and love, which leads to spiritual maturity, brings us more and more deeply into the unity of a common life with Christ as we are progressively assimilated in our whole being to the nature of our Lord" (Vol. 10).

ASSERTIVENESS

1. COMPETITIVE
"The Shark"
WIN/LOSE
"Do it my way, or don't do it at all."
Strategies: compete, control, outwit, preempt, coerce, fight.
Wants others to:
Avoid or Accommodate.
Impatient with dialogue or information-gathering

2. COLLABORATIVE
"The Owl"
WIN/WIN
"My preference is.... What's yours?"
Strategies: gather information, look for alternatives, dialogue, welcome disagreements, focus on interests, not positions.
Wants others to:
Collaborate or Compromise.
Focuses heavily on information-gathering.

3. COMPROMISING
"The Fox"
WIN SOME/LOSE SOME
"I'll back off a little if you do the same."
Strategies: bargain, split the difference, cajole, lower expectations.
Wants others to:
Compromise or Accommodate.
Tolerates exchange of views, but finds it uncomfortable.

4. AVOIDING
"The Turtle"
LOSE/LOSE
"Conflict? What conflict?"
Strategies: flee, avoid, deny, ignore, withdraw, delay, wish.
Wants others to:
Avoid.
Refuses to dialogue or gather information.

5. ACCOMMODATING
"The Teddy Bear"
LOSE/WIN
"Whatever you say...."
Strategies: agree, give in, appease, flatter.
Wants others to:
Fix the issue
Interested in the *other* person's information and approval.

C O O P E R A T I O N

Permission is granted to photocopy this handout for use with this session.

SESSION 3

SAY WHAT!? »»»

» KEY VERSE
Let no evil talk come out of your mouths, but only what is useful for building up, as there is need, so that your words may give grace to those who hear. (Eph. 4:29)

» FAITH STORY
Ephesians 4:25-27, 29–5:2

» FAITH FOCUS
Since the Tower of Babel, communication problems have caused and complicated conflicts. At the same time, the ability to communicate is a magnificent gift from God, and carries with it the potential not only for working through conflicts, but for creating ever deeper levels of human connection and unity.

For the writer of Ephesians it's clear: Poor communication is whatever tears down unity; good communication is whatever is useful for building up. Sometimes that means speaking, and sometimes it means holding our tongue and listening first.

» SESSION GOAL
Help participants learn specific skills for speaking and listening.

» Materials needed and advance preparation
- Paper and pencils or markers
- Chalkboard/chalk or newsprint/markers
- Bibles
- Copies of the handout sheet for Session 3
- Extra copies of the handout sheet from Session 2 (option, see Apply)

TEACHING PLAN

1. FOCUS 5 minutes

» Option A: Pair up. Give each person a sheet of paper and a pencil or marker. Have them sit back to back so they can't see each other's paper. Then have one person in the pair begin to draw a simple design or picture while describing what they are doing. The second person listens and tries to duplicate the design or picture as perfectly as possible by following the instructions of the first person. Switch roles.

Go on to **Option A** in Connect, below.

» Option B: Ask two people to sit in the middle of the large group and go through the exercise above while the rest of the group watches. Switch roles.

Go on to **Option B** in Connect, below.

"Love your enemies and pray for those who persecute you."

Jesus

2. CONNECT 10 minutes

>> **Option A:** When everyone has had a chance to give directions and be the listener, discuss:

1. *How did you feel while the exercise was going on?*
2. *Which was more difficult—giving instructions or trying to follow them?*

>> **Option B:** First let the two who did the exercise talk about it. Ask them:

1. *How did you feel while the exercise was going on?*
2. *Which was more difficult—giving instructions or trying to follow them?*

Then ask the whole group: *What were you thinking or feeling while you were watching this exercise?*

>> **For both options:** Make two columns on a sheet of newsprint or chalkboard. Say something like: *We use this process called "communication" every day to make it possible to live and work and play with other people. Based on the exercise we just did, what are some things that help communication happen?* List the responses in the left column. Then ask: *What are some things that make communication difficult or impossible?* List these in the right column. Share any observations about the two lists.

3. EXPLORE THE BIBLE 15 minutes

Shift to this next activity by saying: *The writer of Ephesians knew the importance of communication in promoting and maintaining unity in the church. Let's see what it looks like.*

Make two columns on a second sheet of newsprint hanging next to the first, or on the remaining half of the chalkboard. Divide into two small groups. Assign the first group to study Ephesians 4:25-27 and 4:29–5:2 and make a list of all the characteristics of **good** communication they can find there. Have them transfer the list to the left column on the newsprint or chalkboard.

Assign the second group to study the same passage and list all the characteristics of **poor** communication. They should transfer their list to the right column.

Invite discussion by having the whole group look at the lists they just made. Ask:

1. *As you compare the lists in the passage, what do you notice?*
2. *Do you see yourself in these lists? Explain.*

Then ask the group to compare the list from scripture with the list they made in Connect. Ask:

1. *How do the lists we made earlier compare to the writer's lists?*
2. *The author of Ephesians was writing to Christians who lived many centuries ago, but how can those lists help us today in our everyday communication: with parents; at school; at work?*

"Communicating means sharing, and sharing demands listening and acceptance. Listening is much more than simply hearing. Hearing is about receiving information, while listening is about communication, and calls for closeness."

Pope Francis

4. APPLY 25 minutes

Distribute copies of the handout sheet and introduce this activity by having the group discuss the "Push and Pull" of good communication. Make sure they understand the concept of balancing **speaking** with **listening** in order to communicate well. Then ask: *Does this remind you of our last session? We talked then about a balance between truth and love, assertiveness and cooperation. How does speaking and listening fit in to all of that?* Help the group connect truth and assertiveness with the "push" of speaking skills; and love and cooperation with the "pull" of listening skills.

Then say something like: *Let's put into action six very practical communication skills you can use every day.*

>>> **Option A** (if you have fewer than 6 people): Go over the task on the handout sheet. Encourage the group to do a role play for each skill on the handout sheet, but you can also simply describe a situation and have each person try the skill.

>>> **Option B** (if you have 6-11 people): Divide into two small groups and assign one small group to the Supportiveness Skills and the other to the Assertiveness Skills. Have them choose how they want to demonstrate the skills (explain in their own words or role play). Allow approximately 8 minutes for the small groups to work; monitor their group work closely, keeping them on their tasks, and letting them know when they have 5 minutes left, 2 minutes left, and then when time is up. Then give each small group 2-3 minutes to present their skills and role plays.

>>> **Option C** (If the group is large enough to divide into six small groups of at least two people in a group): Assign each small group to one of the communication skills on the handout sheet. Explain the options for presentation, and use the time frames outlined in **Option B**, above.

5. RESPOND 5 minutes

Pair up in original two-somes from the Focus activity, and give each person one minute to tell the other (1) which one of the communication skills they think could make a difference in their lives right away, and (2) how or in what situation they will commit to use it in the coming week. Then call the group back together and say something like: *Each of us deals with conflicts every day—some small, some big. Remember that what we say, but especially how we say it, can make all the difference.* Close with prayer.

> "You cannot truly listen to anyone and do anything else at the same time."

M. Scott Peck

LOOK AHEAD

For the next session you will need a ball of red yarn for an exercise focusing on physical and emotional hurts. You will also need a music media player for a game of **Cooperative Musical Chairs**.

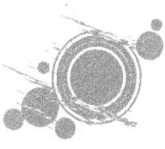

> "Speaking first to be heard is power over. Hearing to bring forth speech is empowering."

Nelle Morton

INSIGHTS FROM SCRIPTURE

This section of Ephesians concerns itself with the responsibility each believer has to contribute to the integrity and stability of the community's life. How? With truthfulness (vs. 25), forgiveness (vv. 26, 32), honesty and philanthropy (vs. 28), and edifying speech (vv. 29, 31).

›› EDIFYING SPEECH

The letter to the Ephesians teaches that edifying speech is whatever builds up, rather than tears down, community. Verse 29 encourages choosing words that will "give grace to those who hear." Verse 31 contrasts communication based on "bitterness and wrath and anger and slander" with that based on kindness, tenderheartedness, and forgiveness.

Such edifying speech, and the ability to treat others with love and respect, springs from gratitude for what God has done for us. God has proved great love for us by sending Jesus to teach us the way of sacrificial love, to call us back onto the path of true life, to live and die for us, and to call us into the community of faith. The community of believers is Christ's Body, a place where, through the Spirit, believers become one Christ as they commune with each other. Therefore, the believers treat each other as God has treated them, for, through Christ, "we are members of one another." (vs. 25)

›› LOVE MAKES COMMUNICATION GO 'ROUND

Life in the community of faith, then, is a life of love, modeled on God's love for us. Diverse people have been brought into unity, and the church has been made one. Since all this was made possible through Love, love should be the basis and motivation for the ways members of the Body relate to each other. One of the first ways the presence or absence of love is revealed in the community is by what comes out of our mouths!

So how important is good communication? The unity of the Body of Christ depends on it! But so does the unity of the world. The world needs good communication skills just as much as the church does. It is up to the Body of Christ to be what Jesus was: teacher and example to the world. Therefore, in everything we do, but especially in the ways we communicate with each other, we need to "be imitators of God, as beloved children, and live in love, as Christ loved us and gave himself up for us, a fragrant offering and sacrifice to God." (Ephesians 5:1-2)

The Push and Pull of Communication

Exploring tough questions facing youth today

Communication is a two-way exchange of information. It involves two seemingly contradictory movements: asserting yourself by speaking—the "push," and supporting another by listening—the "pull." The following skills are easy to learn, and can help you become an expert communicator!

Your task: Explain in your own words what each of the six skills is and why it is important for good communication. **OR** create a brief role play to illustrate its use.

Assertiveness Skills: The "Push" of Speaking

1. **I-Statements:** A clear, nonthreatening way to confront that focuses on oneself rather than on the other person.
   How to use I-Statements:
   - Focus on yourself and your own concern; it's what you have control over: *"I..."*
   - Name the feeling: "I felt *used*..."
   - Name the problem behavior: "I felt used *when you put your name on my work...*"
   - Describe the impact on you: "*...because I put a lot of time into that project.*"

   Why use I-Statements?
   - I take responsibility for my feelings
   - Avoids accusing or blaming the other
   - Reduces defensiveness and de-escalates conflict
   - Expresses strong feelings in a way that values the relationship

2. **Preference Statements:** Communicate clearly your own preferences or desires without stating them as demands, or forcing others to guess. Expressing your preferences invites others to do the same.
   Examples:
   - "My preference is...."
   - "If it were just me...."
   - "What I would like is...."
   - "It would be helpful to me if...."

3. **Purpose Statements:** Communicate clearly what you are trying to accomplish so others don't unknowingly operate at cross-purposes. A purpose statement invites others to respond by questioning your purpose, getting out of your way, or helping you achieve your aim.
   Examples:
   - "What I'm trying to accomplish is...."
   - "I'm hoping to...."
   - "I was going to...."
   - "I'm in the process of...."
   - "My intention is to...."

Supportiveness Skills: The "Pull" of Listening

1. **Paraphrasing:** Reflecting in your own words the essence of what you heard the speaker say.
   How to Paraphrase:
   - Keep the focus on the speaker: "So *you* felt...." "You're saying that...." "What I hear you saying is....is that right?")
   - Re-state in your own words; don't simply parrot the speaker.
   - Reflect both *feeling* and *content* whenever possible: "So you *felt hurt* (**feeling**) when *I forgot your birthday* (**content**)."
   - Be brief, much briefer than the speaker.
   - Match to some extent the emotional intensity of the speaker.

   Why Paraphrase?
   - Demonstrates your commitment to try to understand
   - Clarifies the communication: if you misunderstand, the speaker will correct you
   - Affirms the worth of the speaker and encourages them to say more
   - Reduces defensiveness of both you and the speaker
   - Slows down a fast or angry conversation, helping reduce the intensity of a conflict

2. **Communicating Openness:** This skill helps you clarify the situation before attempting to respond.
   Examples:
   - "Say more about that..."
   - "Spell that out further..."
   - "Tell me what you have in mind..."
   - "Give me a specific example..."

3. **Agreement Stating:** Acknowledging where you agree with the speaker in the midst of a disagreement.
   Examples:
   - "I agree with you that..."
   - "I can see what you're saying about..."
   - "I share your concerns about..."

   Never end an Agreement Statement with "*But....*". Try: "My view is..." "I think...."

Permission is granted to photocopy this handout for use with this session.

SESSION 4

SEND THE VERY BEST: YOURSELF! >>>

>>> KEY VERSE
If another member of the church sins against you, go and point out the fault when the two of you are alone. If the member listens to you, you have regained that one. (Matt. 18:15)

>>> FAITH STORY
Matthew 18:15-17

>>> FAITH FOCUS
Jesus gives us the responsibility to take the lead in seeking reconciliation when we feel offended by another. Sometimes our efforts are rebuffed. Our reaction is often to feel more deeply hurt, to lash out in anger, and to give up.

But Jesus tells us never to give up. Perhaps most importantly, he tells us that we don't have to work through our conflicts alone. Our friends, our church, and Jesus himself are there to help.

>>> SESSION GOAL
Help participants understand how reconciliation happens, and what they can do to help heal a broken relationship.

>>> Materials needed and advance preparation

- Red yarn, several pairs of scissors, masking tape (see Focus)
- Folding chairs, music (*Option A* in Explore)
- Bibles
- Copies of the handout sheet for Session 4
- Paper and pens or pencils

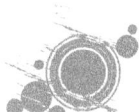 ## TEACHING PLAN

1. FOCUS 10 minutes
Show Off Your Scars. Set out plenty of red yarn, pairs of scissors, and masking tape. Instruct everyone to tie or tape lengths of red yarn on themselves at places that they have been injured in the past. For example, they might tie it around a finger that they cut with a pocket knife, or around their arm where it was broken when they fell off the swing set. Then stand in a circle and invite brief stories about the wounds. For a larger group, divide into small groups of 4 or 5 for this part of the exercise, and then call the groups back into a large circle.

2. CONNECT 10 minutes

Then say something like: *We have been talking about physical hurts. But there are other ways that we can be hurt.* Draw out of the group the realization that hurt feelings and broken relationships are emotional scars that all of us carry with us. Ask: *How are emotional hurts the same as physical hurts? How are they different?* Then invite people to tell about a time when they were emotionally hurt by someone. (Again, divide up if your group is large.) **Note: Be very sensitive to feelings.**

Not everyone needs to share something. Two or three stories will be sufficient to help everyone touch the reality of emotional hurt. Then ask:

1. *In what ways are these stories similar?*
2. *In these stories, where does the pain come from? Why do we care enough to hurt?*
3. *When we have been hurt like this, what can we do about it?*

3. EXPLORE THE BIBLE 10-12 minutes.

Shift to this next activity by having people take their yarn off. Then say: *Let's see what the Bible tells us to do when we have been hurt by someone.*

 Option A: Have the teens in the group play **Cooperative Musical Chairs** (the **group** wins or loses). Set up like traditional musical chairs, with one chair fewer than participants. Play music and stop it suddenly. Everyone is to try to get a seat, but it is the responsibility of the group to *see that everyone has a place to sit*, even if it's on someone's lap! Remove a chair, start again. Remember that in this version, *only* the chairs are eliminated round by round. Everyone sits on however many chairs are left, and it's the responsibility of the group to help everyone stay on. (Stay safe!) If anyone falls off, the *group* loses and must start again at the beginning of the round. Play at least long enough to get the point, and to allow for some creativity in figuring out how to cooperate.

Now read Matthew 18:15-17 by having three people each read a verse. Then ask: *What do this instruction and our game of cooperative musical chairs have to do with each other?* Help the group make the connection between a game that requires everyone to take responsibility to help people stay "on board," and scripture that instructs us to take personal responsibility to try to heal the broken relationship.

Option B: Ask the participants to switch perspectives by thinking of a time when they may have hurt someone else. Tell them to listen to Matthew 18:15-17 from that point of view. Read the passage, then ask:

1. *How would it feel to have the one you hurt come directly to you? What would you be thinking when you see them coming?*
2. *What kind of an approach by them would be most threatening to you?*
3. *What kind of an approach would be most helpful?*
4. *Do you think someone who has hurt you would appreciate having you approach them in that helpful way? Why or why not?*
5. *Are you willing to try it? Why or why not?*

4. APPLY 15-18 minutes

Ask: *Have you ever tried to heal a broken relationship? What happened?* After a brief discussion say: *We're talking about reconciliation: healing a broken relationship. When it comes to reconciliation, there's good news and bad news. The bad news is: It's up to us. When we're hurt, we need to take responsibility for seeking reconciliation. The good news is: It's up to us! We don't have to be helpless victims stuck in our pain. We can choose to take positive action to move toward healing!*

> When it comes to reconciliation, there's good news and bad news. The bad news is: It's up to us. When we're hurt, we need to take responsibility for seeking reconciliation. The good news is: It's up to us! We can choose to take positive action to move toward healing.

Distribute copies of the handout sheet. Take the group through the stages of the **Reconciliation Cycle**. Give time for questions or observations about each stage, and make sure the participants understand reconciliation as a *process*, rather than a *goal*.

Now ask the participants to think of a specific instance when they have been hurt by someone, and to apply the **Reconciliation Cycle** to that situation by writing answers to the key questions at each stage.

5. RESPOND 10 minutes

Mirroring. Ask people to pair up and decide who will be **Person A** and **Person B**. Stand face to face. First, all the As begin to move, slowly and smoothly, and the Bs imitate them as closely as possible. The goal for the As is to be imitated as smoothly as possible, *not* to trick the Bs. After a minute or so, switch roles; the Bs lead and the As imitate. Finally, have no one lead, with the partners simply moving together. Then ask:

1. *In what ways is acting like a mirror like the process of reconciliation outlined in the Reconciliation Circle?*
2. *How did it feel to be leading the movements? To be imitating the movements?*
3. *What was happening when there was no leader? Who was deciding what movements to make?*

Sum up by saying: *Seeking reconciliation is not always easy, but it is always better than living with the pain of brokenness. Sometimes we lead the movements, the other person responds positively, and we find harmony. Sometimes, however, the other person resists our leading, and we switch roles, becoming sensitive to their movements, staying connected in order to respond to their needs and concerns. But all the while we are mirroring the reconciling movement of God's Spirit among us.*

Close with prayer.

INSIGHTS FROM SCRIPTURE

>> A CONFLICT TRANSFORMATION PROCESS

The early church probably put to use these "advanced regulations" as it struggled to cope with internal conflicts. Many understood such a conflict transformation process as keeping in the spirit of Jesus' intention for his followers. Step 1 is to work out the conflict privately, one on one. If that is unsuccessful, step 2 is to take 2 or 3 persons along with you to act as witnesses. This is in keeping with procedures for gathering evidence as outlined in the Hebrew scriptures (see, for example, Deut. 19:15). If that is unsuccessful, the conflict is to be brought before the entire church. If no settlement is reached within the community of faith, the offender is to be treated as a Gentile or tax collector. (This may indeed be a suggestion of excommunication, as most commentaries point out, but it takes on an entirely different meaning when one looks at how Jesus treated Gentiles and tax collectors!)

The church has too often overlooked step 1, and instead used steps 2 and 3 as justification for a legalistic approach to conflict. Step 1 is the essential foundation of all conflict transformation in the faith community, and steps 2 and 3 are to be interpreted in light of it: The church is brought into the process *not* to take it out of the hands of those in conflict, *but to do everything it can do to help them resolve it themselves*. Step 1 calls us to go ourselves to the one who has offended us, *before we do anything else*. This emphasis on

"Think of a conflict as a campfire: Even if all the flames have been put out, the fire will re-ignite if the coals are still hot. You can be sure that if someone isn't satisfied with the way a conflict has been resolved, the conflict may keep 're-igniting.'"

Win/Win Magazine,
by The Peace Education Foundation

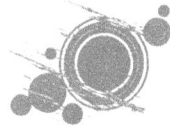

LOOK AHEAD

The next session will involve teaching a simple mediation process and guiding the group in mediation role plays. You may want to find one or two persons from your church or community trained in mediation to assist you.

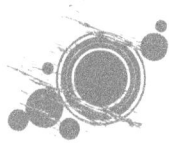

> "The family is the indispensible crucible in which spouses, parents and children, brothers and sisters, learn to communicate and to show generous concern for one another, and in which frictions and even conflicts have to be resolved not by force but by dialogue, respect, concern for the good of the other, mercy and forgiveness."

Pope Francis
Nonviolence: a Style of Politics for Peace, 5 (Message for World Day of Peace 2017).

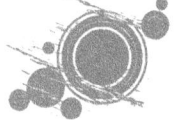

personal responsibility and accountability is in keeping with a great many of Jesus' teachings, especially as found in the Sermon on the Mount (see Matthew 5:1–7:29). Just how important it is in Jesus' thinking to be in right relationship with our brothers and sisters can be seen in his admonition in Matthew 5:23-24: "So when you are offering your gift at the altar, if you remember that your brother or sister has something against you, leave your gift there before the altar and go; first be reconciled to your brother or sister, and then come and offer your gift."

Certainly another relevant teaching by Jesus is on forgiveness. When we go into step 1 without willingness to forgive, we are practically ensuring that it will fail. It's too easy then to hand it off to the church, thus shirking our responsibility. We must be willing to forgive, not just once or twice, or even 7 times, but "seventy-seven times"! (Matthew 18:22). An additional reason to forgive and forgive and forgive: To stay sane after trauma, to survive, we *must* forgive over and over and over, each time the trauma raises its head, writes novelist Diana Gabaldon. Could *this* also be why Jesus said to forgive 70 times 7—for our own health?

LOVING GOD-FACE TO FACE!

Our relationship with our brothers and sisters in the faith community is important because it is a barometer of our relationship with God. As the writer of 1 John puts it: "Those who say 'I love God,' and hate their brothers or sisters, are liars; for those who do not love a brother or sister whom they have seen, cannot love God whom they have not seen. The commandment we have is this: Those who love God must love their brothers and sisters also." (1 John 4:20-21)

THE MINISTRY OF RECONCILIATION

Finally, all this is possible because it is God who brings about reconciliation! Paul proclaims it: "So if anyone is in Christ, there is a new creation: everything old has passed away; see, everything has become new! All this is from God, who reconciled us to himself through Christ, and has given us the ministry of reconciliation." (2 Corinthians 5:17-18)

So what do we do when we find ourselves in conflict with a brother or sister? We love them, and love God, by caring enough to take up the ministry of reconciliation!

> "Reconciliation is about more than righting wrongs and repenting of evildoing. These are surely included, but the understanding of reconciliation in the Christian scriptures sees that we are indeed taken to a new place, a new creation. Reconciliation is not just restoration. It brings us to a place where we have not been before."

Robert J. Schreiter,
Reconciliation

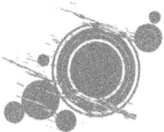

The Reconciliation Cycle

Exploring tough questions facing youth today

STAGE ONE: OPEN RELATIONSHIP
The key to healthy relationships is *risk*. In an open relationship, each person is willing to risk being open with the other. Each risk that results in expectations being met builds trust.
Key Question: How open was I in this relationship?

STAGE TWO: INJURY
At this point in every relationship, a risk results in expectations not being met. The result is injury.
Key Question: With regard to the hurt I am feeling, what expectations were not met?

STAGE THREE: WITHDRAWAL
Withdrawal is a healthy and natural response to injury. Sometimes we withdraw *physically*: turn our back, leave the room, avoid each other. Always we withdraw *emotionally*: we pull back within ourselves to assess the situation. **What happens at this stage determines the outcome.** Our *head* tells us that the "right" thing to do is to make up. So we "reconcile" even though our *heart* isn't in it. We may be back in relationship, but it isn't an open relationship. The indication that true healing has not occurred is that we are no longer willing to *risk* true openness.
Key Question: Am I really ready to risk reconciliation now, or is my head trying to overrule my heart?

STAGE FOUR: SELF-AWARENESS
Self-awareness is needed to move beyond withdrawal. Self-awareness occurs on three levels:
1. We become aware of our emotions, and accept them as valid.
Key Question: What am I feeling when I think about this relationship?
2. We become aware of deep feelings from past hurts that have been brought to the surface by the present injury.
Key Question: When have I felt this way before?
3. We become aware of our own power in the conflict, both in terms of how our actions contributed to the injury, and in terms of the power we have to act positively to bring reconciliation.
Key Question: What impact have I had on this relationship in the past, and what impact can I have on it now?

STAGE FIVE: INTERNAL COMMITMENT TO RECONCILIATION
This is the conscious choice to enter into risk again. It happens when the head says, "It's time," and the heart says, "I'm ready."
Key Question: Am I ready to risk reconciliation?

STAGE SIX: ACT OF RISK
Once the choice has been made to risk again, we can find many opportunities. It is wise to begin with a small risk, for there is a good chance that the other person is not ready yet, and may reject your attempt at reconciliation. Remember that reconciliation is a process, and be ready to risk and risk and risk again.
Key Question: What am I willing to risk in order to work toward reconciliation: What will I say, what will I do?

Based on *From Head to Heart: The Cycle of Reconciliation* by Ron Kraybill
Permission is granted to photocopy this handout for use with this session.

SESSION 5

BE A FRIEND: MEDIATE! >>>

Exploring tough questions facing youth today

>>> KEY VERSE
I urge Euodia and I urge Syntyche to be of the same mind in the Lord. Yes, and I ask you also...help these women....(Philippians 4:2, 3b)

>>> FAITH STORY
Philippians 2:1-5; 4:2-3

>>> FAITH FOCUS
For Paul, unity depends on the ability of people to look beyond their own interests and attend to the needs of others. In this case at Philippi, Euodia and Syntyche needed help resolving their conflict, so Paul called in his "loyal companion" as a mediator.

As Christians we have a responsibility to be open to transform our own conflicts. But we are called to do more. Loving our neighbors sometimes means helping others resolve their conflicts.

>>> SESSION GOAL
Introduce participants to the principle of third party mediation.

>>> Materials needed and advance preparation
- Bibles
- Copies of the handout sheet for Session 5
- Index cards and pencils

TEACHING PLAN

1. FOCUS 10 minutes
Introduce two women from the church at Philippi, Euodia (You-oh´-dee-uh) and Syntyche (Sin´-tih-kee). Explain that these women were having a serious disagreement, and while the Bible doesn't spell out what the issue was, we're going to imagine what it might have been. Then read the following:

> Euodia and Syntyche are both dedicated Christians who do everything they can to contribute to the life of the church at Philippi. They are friends who have worked side by side with the apostle Paul. A highlight for the church are those rare times when Paul himself comes for a visit. The last time Paul was to come, Euodia and her husband offered to have him stay in their home. The church agreed. All in the household were honored, and made extensive preparations for his stay. On the day of Paul's arrival, Euodia was at home

making last-minute preparations. Syntyche and her husband were in the group that welcomed Paul. Paul was obviously tired, and their home was on the way to Euodia's home, so Syntyche invited Paul to stop off for a brief rest. Before she knew it, it was supper time, and it seemed a simple thing to have Paul eat with her family. The conversation was lively until Paul began to yawn. She thought to herself, It seems silly to make Paul get up and travel in the dark to Euodia's house. I'm sure she'll understand if Paul stays here tonight. So she had her servants prepare the guest room, and Paul retired for the night. Meanwhile, Euodia was worrying that Paul had been delayed. She sent a servant to ask one of the church members where he could be. The man said, "Why, he's staying at Syntyche's house. Didn't Euodia know?" The next day, while Paul preached and taught at the church, Euodia pretended that everything was fine. But ever since Paul left that afternoon, she has refused to speak to Syntyche. When Syntyche finally comes to her to find out what's wrong, Euodia's anger comes boiling out.

>> **Option A:** Now have two volunteers play out the confrontation. Instruct Syntyche *not* to give in and apologize. What we want is an angry exchange. Then do some debriefing. Ask each of the role play participants to say how they were feeling at the beginning, during, and at the end of the role play. Ask the group what they were feeling while they watched. Then ask: *Have you ever seen two of your friends fight like this? What was that like? How did you feel?*

>> **Option B:** Now have the group imagine that confrontation between the two women. Ask them to describe it in detail. Then ask: *Have you ever seen two of your friends fight like this? What was that like? How did you feel?*

2. CONNECT 5 minutes

Now ask:

1. *Imagine that Euodia and Syntyche are your friends. Should you do anything? Or is it their problem?*
2. *Have you ever tried to help in a situation like this and gotten into trouble with one or both of your friends because of it? What happened?*

3. EXPLORE THE BIBLE 7-8 minutes

Shift to this next activity by introducing the concept of mediation: *What we have been talking about here is bringing a third person into a conflict between two people in order to help them find their own solution. That's called "mediation." When it is done skillfully, things come out better for everyone.*

Now ask a volunteer to read Philippians 2:1-5 and 4:2-3 out loud. Then ask:

1. *Why can this passage be seen as a call for mediation?*
2. *Who is the third person in this situation?*
3. *What does Paul ask her or him to do?*

Then say: *Now let's learn more about mediation.*

4. APPLY 30 minutes

Distribute copies of the handout sheet. Carefully go over each section on the sheet, giving time for questions. When everyone has a good understanding of the mediation process, move to the following options.

Note: The role plays of a mediation session have been condensed. Have participants use the handout sheet as a guide, but assure them that they will not have to complete every detail; there isn't time in this session. Monitor the role plays carefully, and when it seems that they have captured the essence of a stage, have them "cut" and move forward in the process. Do a quick once-over of the whole process rather than a more thorough job on only part of it.

Option A: Divide into groups of three. Ask each small group to designate a Person 1, a Person 2, and a Person 3. Tell them to remember their number. Explain that they will role play a mediation session with Euodia and Syntyche three times. Each time they will rotate roles, so each person will have a chance to play Euodia, Syntyche, and the "Loyal Companion." Assign their parts for the first round:

Round One: Person 1 — Euodia
Person 2 — Syntyche
Person 3 — The Loyal Companion (Mediator)

Have them take those roles for 4 minutes. Then rotate roles for the second round:

Round Two: Person 1 — The Loyal Companion (Mediator)
Person 2 — Euodia
Person 3 — Syntyche

Role-play for 4 minutes, then rotate again:

Round Three: Person 1 — Syntyche
Person 2 — The Loyal Companion (Mediator)
Person 3 — Euodia

After 4 minutes for the third round, stop the role play, call the group together, and debrief. Ask:

1. *How were you feeling when you were Euodia or Syntyche? Was mediation helpful? Why or why not?*
2. *Was it harder or easier to be the mediator? Why?*

Option B: Do a "fishbowl" mediation role play. Ask for three volunteers to take the roles of Euodia, Syntyche, and The Loyal Companion (Mediator). You may want to have the original Euodia and Syntyche reprise their roles from *Option A* in the Focus activity above. Have the three sit in the middle of the group and role play a mediation session. Depending on how the role play is going, you may want to "freeze" the action to give the group time to analyze what's happening before starting it up again. You may also want to do some Interactive Theater by giving one or two other volunteers the opportunity to step into the role of the Loyal Companion in the middle of the role play. When the role play has been completed, or when time runs out, debrief. Ask the individuals playing Euodia and Syntyche: *How did you feel during the mediation? Was mediation helpful?* Then ask the mediator(s): *How did it feel to be the mediator? What was the easy part? What was the hard part?* Finally ask the group: *What did you see happening in this role play? Do you think mediation was helpful?*

Option C: Have the group discuss briefly how a mediation session might go with Euodia, Syntyche, and the Loyal Companion. Then ask them to imagine that they are The Loyal Companion, and have just successfully completed the mediation session with Euodia and Syntyche. Have them compose an e-mail or a text message to Paul explaining what happened in the session and describing the solution to the conflict. Encourage them to include details: Where did they meet? How long did it take? When did the "breakthrough" happen? Then ask for volunteers to read their messages to the group. Discuss the insights.

NOTE

This session is not intended to qualify anyone as a trained mediator. It is merely an introduction. Use Options and Contacts in the **Extender Session** to augment mediation skills, and encourage participants to take advantage of mediation training in your area.

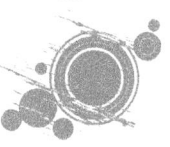

TOP FIVE ADVANTAGES OF MEDIATION

1. You won't get beaten up! Mediation provides a safe, non-hostile environment to talk out a problem.
2. It's completely confidential. You can admit you were acting like a total jerk—no one will ever know!
3. You might actually learn something. Talking about feelings and perceptions helps you to understand the other person's position. You'll begin to see the other person as a person, not as "the enemy."
4. It's free!
5. It really works. In mediation, no one loses. No one tells you what to do. Since you and the other person voluntarily discuss the issue, the solution is your solution.

The Peace Education Foundation
www.peace-ed.org/

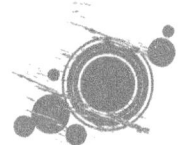

5. RESPOND 7-8 minutes

Option A: Hand out index cards and pencils. Ask each participant to think of two of their friends who are or have been in conflict with each other. Then ask them to think about whether they would be willing to offer Friendship Mediation, and if so, how they would ask them. Have them write on the card what they might say to their friends to tell them about mediation and to offer to help them resolve their conflict. When everyone is finished, say something like: *All of us have friends who sometimes don't get along with each other. Because we are their friend, it hurts us when they hurt each other. Take this card to remind yourself that with Friendship Mediation we don't have to sit back and feel helpless. We can be a friend; we can mediate!*
Close with prayer.

Option B: Encourage participants to try Friendship Mediation with elementary-age kids. What would the mediator's scenario look like on a playground? As a group, write it out:

Conflict: Two kids are rolling in the dirt fighting.

Conflict: One kid comes to you in tears, complaining that another pushed them out of the swing.

Think of one or two other playground conflicts. Decide as a group how you might mediate them.

Close in prayer, addressing Christ as the Great Mediator, asking for wisdom and compassion in learning to mediate.

INSIGHTS FROM SCRIPTURE

The situation is one we could find in any faith community today. We don't know for certain what caused the dispute, but the conflict between Euodia and Syntyche was apparently serious enough, or long-standing enough, to cause Paul some concern. Note, however, that Paul does not scold the women, or try to make them feel guilty for the conflict. He doesn't launch into a long lecture on how conflict is bad, or un-Christian. No, for Paul conflict was a given, a natural part of life. The issue is not *whether* there is conflict, but *what you do about it*.

IS MEDIATION A MODERN THING?

Though focus on conflict transformation as a specific field of study and practice is relatively new, the *principles* of mediation, what makes it work, have been around for a long time. It's clear that Paul knew about them. In his letter to the Philippians, he addresses Euodia and Syntyche directly and by name, something he rarely did, asking them to "be of the same mind in the Lord" (Philippians 4:2). But then he calls for mediation of their dispute! He asks his "loyal companion" to help Euodia and Syntyche work out their disagreement. What Paul is calling for could be called "friendship mediation." We don't know who this "loyal companion" was, but the phrase literally means "in the same yoke." This companion had worked side by side with Paul, and with the two women. Their friendship and shared faith was the foundation upon which reconciliation could be built.

A REMARKABLE EXAMPLE

Paul's call for mediation is remarkable simply as an example of mediation in the early church. But it is even more remarkable when we realize what Paul *could* have called for but didn't. He could have simply taken an authoritarian approach and either pronounced his own judgment, imposing a solution on Euodia and Syntyche, or he could have asked his "loyal companion" to do it. Instead, he respected and trusted the two women enough to leave the responsibility for a solution in their hands, and simply asks another member of the church to assist them. (This is more remarkable still if the "true companion" was, like Paul, a man; the implied gender equality would have been found nowhere else in the ancient world.) There is one more remarkable thing—how seldom churches today follow this example! Our parishes, too, would greatly benefit from members trained in friendship mediation, people who are willing to use it to resolve their disagreements.

A THEOLOGY OF MEDIATION

Paul's call for mediation was more than a means of conflict transformation. It was an expression of his theology. In Philippians 2:1-5 he urges the members of the church to "be of the same mind, having the same love, being in full accord and of one mind" (vs. 2). This was a tall order then, as it is today. If Paul believed that such unity depended on our own human capabilities, he probably wouldn't have bothered calling for it. Today we call that "pragmatism"—dealing with things "the way they are," rather than the way we wish things were. But Paul tirelessly proclaimed his faith that the church is Christ's Body, and that through Christ we can be *more* than we are!

Moreover, he understood Christ to be not just *a* mediator, but *the* Mediator. He would have resonated with the words from 1 Timothy: "For there is one God; there is also one mediator between God and humankind, Christ Jesus, himself human, who gave himself a ransom for all" (1 Tim. 2:5-6a). The reason for Christ's sacrificial death on the cross, and the meaning of his resurrection, was to make peace once and for all between God and people.

MEDIATION TRANSFORMS THE BELOVED COMMUNITY...

For Paul, the fact of Christ's mediating role has real and practical implications for the faith community. First, it helps us see and understand Christ's ongoing power to transform our life together. A tremendous example for Paul and the early church was the way Christ opened the church to the non-Jews. There had been centuries of enmity between Jews and Gentiles, and the first serious controversy in the early church was whether Gentiles were welcome in the fellowship. How did that controversy turn out? "But now in Christ Jesus you who once were far off have been brought near by the blood of Christ. For he is our peace; in his flesh he has made both groups into one and has broken down the dividing wall, that is, the hostility between us.... So he came and proclaimed peace to you who were far off and peace to those who were near; for through him both of us have access in one Spirit to the Father" (Eph. 2:13-14, 17-18). In Christ there are no enemies; the church is open to all!

...BY TRANSFORMING OUR RELATIONSHIPS

When Paul urges us to "let the same mind be in you that was in Christ Jesus" (Phil. 2:5), he is calling believers to be peacemakers, as Christ is. He asks his "loyal companion" to be a mediator between Euodia and Syntyche. He asks us, too, to "look not to your own interests, but to the interests of others" (Phil. 2:4). But the only way Paul can ask such difficult things is through his complete confidence in the mediating power of Christ's living presence. *We* don't make peace; *Christ,* the Great Mediator, makes peace through us.

> "You can't make people be who they don't want to be yet. You just be gentle and let them get there by themselves."
>
> Brian Doyle,
> *The Plover*

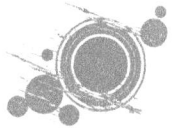

Friendship Mediation

In Real Life — Exploring tough questions facing youth today

When a third friend helps two friends stop fighting and find agreement

STEP 1: INTRODUCTION

1. Explain the process.
2. Set ground rules: No interrupting! No name-calling or threatening!

STEP 2: STORYTELLING

(A "talking stick" or other object could be helpful; only the person holding it is allowed to talk at that moment.)

1. Ask one person to tell what happened and how they are feeling about it. Ask the other person to be patient, and assure them that they will get a turn.

   Mediator's Role: Have them talk to you, not the other person.

   Paraphrase what they are saying, and sum up what you heard. Let them correct you if you heard wrong or missed something.

2. Ask the second person to tell what happened and how they are feeling about it.

   Mediator's Role: Same as for the first person.

STEP 3: PROBLEM-SOLVING

1. Define the problem.

   Mediator's Role: You can try one of two approaches:
   - Either state the problem yourself: *"It sounds like the problem is that…. Is that right?"*
   - Or ask the two of them: *"From what you have heard, what does the problem seem to be?"*

   Make sure both agree on what the problem is before moving on. You will know they are ready to move on when the fighting stops and the problem-solving begins.

2. Solve the problem.

   Mediator's Role: Have them talk to each other now.
   - Ask: **"What are some possible solutions to the problem?"**
   - Encourage them to **brainstorm** as many solutions as they can *first*; then and only then have them begin to **evaluate** the solutions.
   - Listen for **positions:** *"I insist on…." "The only thing I'll accept is…."* Translate into **interests** by saying: *"Say why that is important to you."*

STEP 4: AGREEMENT

1. Agree on a solution.

   Mediator's Role: Listen for any area of agreement and point it out: *"It sounds like you agree that…."*
   - Write out the agreement: *"We agree that…."*
   - Help make it **specific:** Who will do what, when, where?
   - Make sure the agreement is **balanced** (meets the needs of both persons) and **nonjudgmental**. For example: *"We agree to share."* **Not:** *"We agree that Bill will stop being selfish."*

2. Sign the agreement.
3. Shake hands, hug—**celebrate!**

TIPS FOR MEDIATORS

- **Remember, it's their problem!** You don't need to come up with a solution for them. They can do that. After all, they are the experts on their own conflict!
- **Stay neutral.** You may feel that one person is right and the other is wrong, but let them work it out.

(Adapted from: *Mediation and Facilitation Training Manual: Foundations and Skills for Constructive Conflict Transformation*)

EXTENDER SESSION
(Best used after Session 5)

PRACTICAL MEDIATION

SESSION GOAL
Help participants better understand the practical application of the mediation process and gain more practice in third-party mediation.

SESSION ACTIVITIES:

Option A: Invite someone from your parish who either has experience in being a mediator or who has had a conflict mediated by a third party. Ask them to share with the group about their experiences—the successes and failures, how they felt, etc. If the person is qualified, they might also help the group practice their mediation skills.

Option B: Contact the restorative justice office of your diocese or one of the organizations listed on the right and ask for a list of possible speakers/workshop leaders in your area on the topic of conflict resolution. Invite the leader for a session, asking them to focus primarily on practicing mediation skills.

HELPFUL CONTACTS

Catholic Mobilizing Network
415 Michigan Ave. NE,
Suite 210, Washington,
D.C. 20017
202-541-5290
CatholicsMobilizing.org

Pace e Bene Nonviolence Service
510-268-8765
PaceEBene.org

Mennonite Conciliation Service
21 S 12th St
Akron, PA 17501-0500
707-859-3889
E-mail: mcs@mccus.org
www.mcc.org/mcs.html

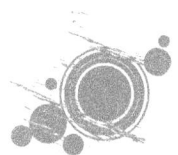

MEDIATION RESOURCE

Here's a link to a concise summary of the overall mediation process: http://store.peaceeducation.org/images/MEP2-Large.jpg.

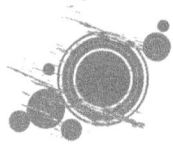

Qualities (of a mediator) include:

- Spiritual centeredness, self-awareness, and self-control
- Ability to be assertive and clear without being harsh—firm and gentle at the same time
- Ability to keep an open spirit and listen well, even when tensions are high
- Willingness to move toward conflict rather than away from it
- Awareness of how one's presence (posture, proximity, gestures, tone of voice) affects others, and ability to use presence in a helpful way
- Ability to adapt to changing situations while keeping primary purposes in mind
- Ability to work as part of a team as well as on one's own

Skills to bring or learn:

- Listening skills
- Speaking skills (for example, paraphrasing, reframing)
- Sensitivity to nonverbal communication
- Problem-solving skills
- Negotiation skills
- Strategies to defuse anger/aggression
- Ability to scan crowds and identify people needing assistance
- Ability to project confidence and positive, calming presence
- Ability to deal with fear and other feelings
- Ability to make themselves heard and seen (for example through voice, tone, bodily posture, clothing, presence)
- Ability to discern how/when to stay out of certain conflicts

CLUELESS AND CALLED
Discipleship and the Gospel of Mark

What does it take to be a disciple? This study of the Gospel of Mark focuses on the requirements for following Jesus' way and the abundant life that is ours as a result. (5 sessions)

DO MIRACLES HAPPEN?
Signs and Wonders in the Gospel of John

The greatest miracle, recorded in John 1:14 and 3:16, is the miracle of God's love that became flesh and lived among us. But John also included examples of what we more traditionally think of as miracles: the wonder of abundance from little; healing; signs of impossibility and faith; and the resurrection. (5 sessions)

DO THE RIGHT THING
Ethics Shaped by Faith

How do you know what's right and what's wrong? Even when you figure it out, the right thing is often the unpopular or unpleasant choice. This unit offers participants a clearer sense of what it means to claim a faith identity, a foundation that can help them sort out the gritty details of ethics shaped by faith. (6 sessions)

FIGHT RIGHT
A Christian Approach to Conflict Resolution

This unit will help youth understand conflict and its function. They will learn how they can be honest and loving, and explore how conflict can be used for positive results. They will also learn ways to enhance their communication skills. 1 Corinthians. (5 sessions)

GOD IS A WARRIOR?
Violence in the Bible

The Bible challenges us to be reconciled to one another and work for justice. So what do we do with the stories that seem to condone violence or even encourage it? A discussion of issues in the Old and New Testaments. (6 sessions)

HOW DO YOU KNOW?
Wisdom in the Bible

Wisdom literature teaches us that we gain knowledge of the world, ourselves, and God through experience and observation. This unit provides practical, hands-on wisdom to help young people avoid life's snares and grow closer to God. Proverbs, Job, Ecclesiastes. (5 sessions)

HOW TO BE A TRUE FRIEND
The Bible Reveals Friendship's Heart

To be a friend takes skill. Help youth discover the secrets of friendship through various stories from the Old and New Testament. (6 sessions)

HOW TO READ THE BIBLE
Building Skills for Bible Study

What kind of book is the Bible? What does this book mean to me? This unit looks at the Bible as revelation, as history, as literature. Selected scripture. (5 sessions)

KEEPING THE GARDEN
A Faith Response to God's Creation

If Christians believe that God made the world, we do not need any more compelling reason to care for it than that God has handed us a treasure to hold and protect. This unit gets beyond trendy environmentalism and challenges youth to see environmental awareness as a religious issue. Genesis. (6 sessions)

MANTRAS, MENORAHS, AND MINARETS
Encountering Other Faiths

How is Christianity different from other faiths? Why do others believe the way they do? This study can give youth a new appreciation for the uniqueness of Jesus. Selected scripture. (5 sessions)

SALT, LIGHT, AND THE GOOD LIFE
The Beatitudes and the Sermon on the Mount

What can youth expect in a life of discipleship? This unit explores the Sermon on the Mount under four main sections: the Beatitudes, Salt and Light, Jesus and the Law, and Heavenly Teachings. Matthew 5. (6 sessions)

A SPECK IN THE UNIVERSE
The Bible on Self-Esteem and Peer Pressure

Discover God's unconditional love and acceptance of all people. This study will show positive ways to have one's life make a difference, and help youth find ways to resist negative peer pressure and turn it into positive action. (6 sessions)

THE RADICAL REIGN
Parables of Jesus

Jesus used parables to reveal what the kingdom of God is like, and how God relates to us. This study highlights how the parables reveal God's reign as radically different from the world we live in, and what that means for the Christian life. (6 sessions)

TESTING THE WATERS
Basic Tenets of Faith

Discover the biblical roots for the central Christian concepts of covenant, community, and baptism. This short course is a way to test the (baptismal) waters of Christianity before diving in, or review the basics for those who already have. (6 sessions)

WHO IS GOD?
Engaging the Mystery

God is beyond human comprehension, yet desires to be known. These sessions focus on the way we get clues about and glimpses of God from the Bible, God's creation, and church tradition. Selected scripture. (5 sessions)

www.ingramcontent.com/pod-product-compliance
Lightning Source LLC
Chambersburg PA
CBHW080409170426
43193CB00016B/2861